Transforming Negative Emotions

Also by the Author

This Mystery and I

The Quiet Place Within

Talks With Temerlen

The Little Book of Awareness

The Heart of Awareness

Inside the Mind of Awareness

Transforming Negative Emotions

Peter Ingle

Transforming Negative Emotions

Transforming Negative Emotions

Copyright © 2008–2022 by Peter Ingle
All Rights Reserved

No part of this publication may be reproduced, store, or transmitted, in any form, or by any means, electronic, mechanical, photocopying, recording, or otherwise, without permission in writing from the author.

Library of Congress Cataloging-in-Publication Data

Ingle, Peter M.
Transforming Negative Emotions

ISBN 978-0-9746349-1-3
Produced in the United States

CONTENTS

About This Book i

An Introduction to the Fourth Way 1

The Nature of Negative Emotions 41

The Role of Non-Expression 57

Negative Emotions and Denying Force 71

The Process of Transformation 83

Transformation and Awareness 103

Transforming Negative Emotions

About This Book

Comprehensive knowledge about what negative emotions are, the role they play in human psychology, and the possibility of transforming them as a bridge to higher consciousness belongs to a system of ideas known as the Fourth Way. These ideas were introduced to the western world in the early twentieth century by G.I. Gurdjieff, a Greek-Armenian living in Russia. The 'system' as he called it was later organized in written form by his protégé, P.D. Ouspensky, a Russian author who had gained notoriety through the publication of two early works: *The Fourth Dimension* and *Tertium Organum*.

One of Ouspensky's subsequent books, *In Search of The Miraculous*, tells how he met and studied with Gurdjieff. Another book, *The Fourth Way*, comprises questions and answers from meetings that Ouspensky held in London and New York from 1921–1945. He also wrote *The Psychology of Man's Possible Evolution* which is a condensation of fourth way ideas.

The material that follows on these pages is drawn from my observations and insights over 40 plus years of studying the system. All the observations revolve around three main points: (1) the underlying nature of negative emotions, (2) the benefits gained by not expressing them, and (3) how non-expression is related to transformation, which is a separate 'step'. Underlying all of these is the consciousness of awareness.

Prior to the twentieth century, the idea of transformation was a mysterious process veiled in the ancient idea of alchemy under a notion of transmuting the 'coarse' into the 'fine'—which of course is an internal, not external, process.

The foundation of this process is withholding the expression of negative emotions, but this needs to be understood in the right way. It is not a matter of simply not expressing negative emotions. It is a matter of knowing how the *physical* lever of non-expression acts as a *psychological* catalyst that can fuel conscious awareness.

In right order, 'withholding' the expression of negative emotions—particularly under the duress of intense suffering—enables awareness to 're-member itself' (to become aware of being aware) *above* negative emotions and thereby transcend the sense of self which negative emotions spring from. The more this is understood, the more conscious transformation becomes and the deeper awareness expands as the mystery of itself.

As Ouspensky said, "You cannot struggle with negative emotions without remembering yourself more, and you cannot remember yourself more without struggling with negative emotions. If you remember these two things, you will understand everything better."

To fully comprehend what he meant, it is best to start with a brief overview of how these two ideas form the core of the psychological side of the fourth way system.

An Introduction to the Fourth Way

THE FOURTH WAY, which is said to have existed for millennia, is based on a system of ideas that describe human psychology as a platform and vehicle for conscious awareness. According to George Gurdjieff who introduced these ideas to the west, the fourth way appears and disappears depending on the religious and political climate of the times.

The fourth way derives its name from the fact that it is distinct from three 'traditional' ways of inner development that were more common in the east: the way of the fakir, the way of the monk, and the way of the yogi.

The way of the fakir is an approach to conscious awareness through mastering the physical body by overcoming pain and enduring instinctive hardship.

The way of the monk is an approach to conscious awareness through mastering the emotions, typically in the form of religious devotion.

The way of the yogi is an approach to conscious awareness through mastering the intellect, a main stay of which is meditation.

Each of these three ways—each intended for different types of people—is a vehicle, a conduit, and a pathway to conscious awareness. All three characteristically require withdrawal into a monastery or ashram or secluded place.

The fourth way, on the other hand, takes place, not in isolation or under special circumstances, but in the ordinary conditions of contemporary daily life. It is said to be a balanced way of transcending the body, the emotions, and the mind *at the same time* through *direct* work on conscious awareness.

But what does this really mean? What is conscious awareness? How does it appear? How do we recognize it? And most importantly, how does it recognize and realize itself?

Degrees of Consciousness

The fourth way explains that the consciousness of awareness can manifest in four successive degrees or levels. Although awareness itself does not change, it experiences degrees of opaqueness and clarity, variations of contraction and expansion, and a wide spectrum of self-awareness—from no cognition of itself as awareness to full self-realization within the universe. In fourth way language, these fluctuations of degree are referred to as states of consciousness.

The first level or 'state' of consciousness is the condition of being asleep at night when all but the barest sensations are dimmed and awareness resides in the *instinctive world of dreams* and is, for the most part, oblivious to the outside world. In this state of consciousness dreams are our reality.

When we wake up from sleep in the morning, awareness expands into the second state of consciousness which is a higher dimension that encompasses the *physical world of activity* where we walk, talk, have thoughts, feel emotions, make decisions, and accomplish tasks. This is our reality in the 'second' state. The dimension of the first state is still there *inside the second state.* It is simply dimmed by the brighter light of earthly impressions and human activity.

In this waking state, awareness often fluctuates throughout both the first (dream) and second (waking) states of consciousness. One moment we are attentive to the task at hand, the next moment we are daydreaming about the past or future. Then a noise or the sound of a person's voice 'brings us back' to what we are doing. Typically, however, we take little note of these fluctuations of awareness, nor do we control them in any way. Even less do we realize that there is a possibility of greater awareness above and beyond these two states of consciousness.

The fourth way explains that the third state is elusive to our perception, partly because we think we are already in it, and partly because we don't realize that it exists as a higher dimension than thought. When we hear that it is a state of heightened awareness, we assume we can just raise the level of our awareness whenever we choose. Although it is true that we can voluntarily focus our attention, what we don't understand is that this is not conscious awareness. It is simply focused attention. A key ingredient is still missing.

In the third state of consciousness, awareness experiences a more vivid view of the world. We see everything in a simple and clear way, sometimes in a more poetic or mystical way. At the same time, there is a detached sense of awareness that seems to stand apart from and *outside* whatever it sees. This may happen, for example, when we find ourselves in new surroundings, or when something unexpected happens, or when we are in the presence of great natural beauty such as Niagara Falls, the Grand Canyon, the Alps, or a spectacular view of earth from a jet airliner. Suddenly, awareness is rendered more conscious, more present, more awake, and we become more aware of ourselves as the pure witness of our surroundings. The key point is that awareness becomes aware of observing from a higher dimension of consciousness that is aware of being aware as a distinct quality of inner presence and calm.

We normally experience our life from a low state of awareness and spend most of our waking moments in the first and second states with occasional flashes of the third state, but these flashes can pass almost unnoticed without their significance being fully realized. At the same time, it is possible to experience more moments of life from the dimension of a higher state of conscious awareness.

According to the fourth way, only through intense or prolonged experiences within the third state can awareness comprehend its true nature, and only then can we start to fathom what it would mean *to be* full conscious awareness.

As we gain conscious command of awareness (more accurately, as it gains command of itself), there comes the possibility of expansion into still another state of consciousness—the 'fourth' state—which is a broader, deeper, higher dimension of awareness. The fourth state is the ultimate mystical nirvana which people have sought for centuries, yet the fourth way teaches that it is reached by awareness passing *through* the third state. This is why the central purpose and sole aim of the fourth way is to free awareness from the psychological grips that keep it ensconced in the lower dimension of the second state.

Awareness 'Remembering' Itself

The foundation of the fourth way system is that we are usually unaware of ourselves; that no one is automatically conscious of himself; that no one 'remembers' himself. The seemingly simple fact of being aware of our own existence does not occur to us. To put it more succinctly, awareness is not usually *conscious* of being aware. Just stop for a moment and think about that: we exist in human form on a planet in a solar system in a vast universe and are, for the most part, unaware of our own awareness of this fact.

Even if a person is told about this and sincerely tries to be more consciously aware, they soon forget to be aware of—to 'remember'—their own existence. Awareness *unknowingly* falls asleep again and everything goes on as before—in a dim state of awareness that shuts out the larger picture of our existence as humans *inside* a planet that is in turn *inside* a solar system *within* a galaxy that is itself *inside* a vast universe.

Of course, everyone is aware of their existence to some degree, but it is small compared to what is possible. For the most part, everyone takes their existence—particularly their awareness of existence—for granted. No one remembers about his existence on purpose. Quite the contrary: everyone is always forgetting themselves one moment to the next.

One of the curiosities of the third state of consciousness is that even when we know about it, we cannot access it with the body or mind. We have to find a different way because what we are looking for exists outside the body and mind as a higher dimension of awareness.

On the fourth way, the primary preparation for this is a practice called self-remembering. Self-remembering is a conscious effort to be aware of yourself in your surroundings as often as possible. It means holding attention on the realization of yourself being aware, while simultaneously being aware of either your outer world (where you are and what you are doing) or your inner world (of thoughts, feelings, and sensations), *or both at the same time.* In this way you become aware of whatever you are observing in the moment *while remaining aware as the observer.*

For instance, right now it is possible to be aware of these printed words *and* be aware of yourself reading them, while *also* being aware of being aware of yourself reading them. These two extra dimensions of awareness—especially the latter—never happen by themselves. And without them awareness always slips into ordinary, one-dimensional attention.

The other key point to understand about self-remembering is that it is not a physical or mental or emotional 'effort'. It is a wordless presence of awareness that resides beyond the brain, above the mind, outside the body. It is simply awareness.

Imagination

Conscious awareness—being aware of being aware—is indeed the magic potion for anyone seeking the nirvana of higher consciousness. Yet, simple as it is, it is elusive because of tendencies in our psychology which divert awareness away from itself, *into* our psyche, *into* our body, and *into* the events of our life. In other words, awareness has a propensity to slip out of the metaphysical dimension of itself and be *appropriated by* lower dimensions of our mind, body, and physical life.

One of these psychological tendencies is called imagination. In fourth way terminology, imagination means random associations, daydreaming, thoughts about the future or the past, and supposing (imagining) things about ourselves and other people. A person with his gaze 'fixed' in thought is in imagination. Awareness of himself and his environment is absent, entirely absorbed by the inner workings of imagination. Although the person is physically in the waking state of consciousness, he has psychologically lapsed into the realm of dreams. But he does not see any harm in this, partly because it is so satisfying to be in imagination, and partly because it has never been pointed out as a diversion from conscious awareness.

Another example of imagination is when we are looking at a scene or listening to an idea and then start to think about—to imagine—a similar scene or similar idea. Instead of seeing or hearing what is in front of us, we associate to something else and see that *in our imagination.* We do not realize that awareness *becomes whatever we are imagining.* In other words, as awareness loses consciousness of itself, it disappears into the clouds of imagination where it 'falls asleep'.

Imagination also takes other forms, such as glib talking, talking to oneself, being physically 'busy', and even eating frantically or in a trance-like state.

When we first hear about imagination, we perhaps see it as the exception to our normally alert state of mind. We do not see that it is the rule; that imagination *interferes* with almost every moment of life; that, unbeknownst to us, we even imagine who we are and how we appear to others.

But if we hear about conscious awareness and try to remember ourselves—to be aware of being aware—we may begin to see that we "forgot to remember ourselves." This realization can start to reveal what it might mean to become fully aware of our existence.

Identification

Awareness is easily lured into imagination because of a second psychological tendency called identification, which is what happens to us when a person, object, or interest captivates awareness, draws it out of self-awareness, and embodies it in the thing it has become aware of.

A cat chasing a mouse is identified. So is a person intent on a task, insisting on a point of view, immersed in anxiety, mesmerized by another person, or consumed by a television or computer screen or smartphone. In all these cases, awareness surrenders itself and *grants identity to* the object of its interest.

The problem is that we have come to view identification, not as a loss of awareness, but as interest and enthusiasm, as focus and dedication. Being identified is considered normal, useful, and necessary. To be without identification is to be listless, dull, unproductive, boring. The fourth way, however, explains that the reverse is true: that identification robs us of our real identity; that it is the *exact opposite* of conscious self-awareness.

Another thing which happens as a result of identification is that our imaginary sense of 'I' grows more concentrated and stronger. But a part of us likes this feeling and fails to see the damaging effect it has on awareness.

Internal Considering

A third tendency that diverts awareness from being aware of being aware is our identification with other people. The fourth way refers to this as internal considering, or 'inner-considering'. Inner-considering happens when we worry about what other people think about us: whether they notice us, admire us, approve of us, and respect us, or whether we suspect they might be ridiculing us behind our backs. Inner-considering is also behind the anxiety that prompts us to adjust our hair before entering a room, or to scratch our head when we are unsure of our response to a question. Sometimes it can cause overwhelming nervousness and fear to the extent that we cannot speak to another person or express ourselves in front of a group.

Inner-considering may also take the opposite form of imagining that we are not considering other people enough; that we are not treating *them* with enough respect or courtesy or admiration; that we don't ever quite meet *their* expectations and requirements—in which case we may deprecate ourselves, feel sorry for ourselves, or feel guilty that we are the cause of someone else's problem.

Being mired in internal considering comes from evaluating our life in relation to ourselves, which is why it is called *internal* considering. It produces a distorted, self-centric point of view that consumes enormous energy *at the expense of* conscious awareness.

One of the best ways to heighten awareness is to turn the psychology of inner-considering around and see ourselves, not as the center of things, but as part of a larger whole. This means seeing other people, not in terms of our need for approval or their need for recognition, but according to the needs of the larger whole or situation in which we find ourselves.

Turning internal considering around like this is called 'external considering'. External considering means thinking of others, not in terms of us, but in terms of their circumstances, their needs, their 'requirements'. External considering can also be seen as a form of imitating conscious awareness which is, by its nature, cognizant of its relation to the larger universe and *its purposes, its needs, its reality.*

Negative Emotions

Our most catastrophic diversion from conscious awareness is the tendency to outwardly express the many negative emotions that form as a psychological cocktail of imagination, identification, and inner-considering. Simply put, by means of imagination, identification, and inner-considering, we *conclude* that other people and circumstances conspire to make us negative; that *they* are the cause of our negativity or suffering. Through a series of well-oiled mental adjustments, we *justify* our accusations, indulge in them with pleasure, feel an urge to vent their buildup of energy, and then *allow* ourselves to express that energy in the form of irritation, opposition, argument, self-pity, self-righteousness, vindication, anger—and more.

The spectrum of negative emotions comprises a long list that also includes things like impatience, agitation, judgment, gossip, holding a grudge, anxiety, worry, suspicion, indignation, hatred, resentment, depression, guilt, and fear.

From a young age we are taught—through imitation and social pressure—that the outward expression of negative emotions is a harmless release of energy and even a necessary show of character. After all, it seems that someone or something has *made* us negative, that the cause of our negativity lies outside of us, and that we have a right to accuse, blame, voice our complaint, and get it "off our chest."

The fourth way turns all this rationale upside-down by explaining that the cause of *all* negativity is not external, but internal; that negative emotions are a by-product of the wrong view we have of ourselves and others, of the world in general, and of the role of suffering in our life. From this perspective, expressing negative emotions is never useful, never necessary, and never a sign of strength. On the contrary, it is always a sign of weakness; it is due to emotional immaturity and shortsighted thinking; it is pointless in itself and completely unnecessary; and, above all, it is detrimental to awareness.

The primary reason that negative emotions are so harmful is that the 'substance' of conscious awareness is *burned* through the psychological manufacture and physical expression of negative emotions. In this process, negative emotions *reject* reality by *denying* awareness its rightful opportunity to see things as they really are.

This understanding is veiled, however, by the psychological machinations that produce a negative emotion. For example, if we could watch a negative emotion unfold in slow motion, we would see it start as an instinctive 'itch', become a psychological impulse, coalesce as a definitive sense of self, pass through a labyrinth of reinforcing attitudes, inflate as a surging emotion, and finally seek release through verbal and physical expression. In actuality, however, this elaborate, multi-stage process unfolds at lightning speed and is nearly impossible to witness *even* when we know to look for it.

Understanding the maze of negative emotions, being able to trace them to their roots, learning to corral them before they coalesce, being able to withhold their expression, and understanding what transformation means—all of this requires a new kind of study and a new command of awareness. It also requires a readiness to confront our deepest notion of 'I' with the knowledge that expressing negative emotions bolsters our feeling of 'I' while not expressing negative emotions disarms it.

Ironically, ordinary psychology does everything to reinforce and reassure our notion of 'I'. In striking contrast, the fourth way gradually disassembles it, dissolves the illusion behind it, and opens a door to the higher dimension of conscious awareness.

The Many 'I's

Science, religion, education, and psychology portray man as having full consciousness, unity, and will. After all, we appear to be conscious, to have an individual self, and to control our actions. The fourth way views all of these traits in a different light by explaining that our actions are involuntary responses to outside stimuli and that we are in a very real sense puppets manipulated by visible and invisible influences in each moment that act upon us and compel us into action.

Our actions are the result of thoughts that are governed, not by the 'brain' as we know it, but by four independent brains which the fourth way calls 'centers': the intellectual center, emotional center, moving center, and instinctive center. Each of these four centers has its own means of perceiving, responding to, and recording events, but the distinction between centers is imperceptible until we start looking for them with the light of conscious awareness. Even then it is challenging because all four centers work in tandem to produce an appearance of continuity in our actions and a core sense of 'I' behind them. Backstage, however, our inner world is a continuous chain of 'I's produced by the different centers: I am hungry, I am full, I am happy, I am sad, I want, I don't like, I think, I hate, I know, I can, I never can, and so on *ad infinitum*.

We are usually not cognizant of all these 'I's constantly replacing and contradicting each other. We are not cognizant, partly because we have never studied ourselves in this way, and partly because awareness pulses at such a low level that it is usually *unaware of itself as the awareness* that is separate from *all* the 'I's in our psychological world. Instead of being aware of itself *above* that world, awareness attaches itself to each 'I' that appears in the moment. It literally *becomes* each 'I' produced by the four centers, without recognizing that the 'I's are one thing and that it—awareness—is an unseen 'something else' which exists beyond the 'I's.

Four Lower Centers

The purpose of the fourth way is to guide the self-realization of conscious awareness, but awareness is difficult to understand at first because it is not thought, feeling, movement, or sensation. To realize this, we need to study awareness in terms of *what it is not* by learning to recognize the four lower centers, the endless chain of 'I's produced by them, and the artificial sense of a single 'I' behind them. Observing ourselves in this way reveals that awareness resides *outside* the four centers as the observer behind observing, the seer behind seeing, the pure awareness aware of being aware of everything else. Realizing this requires a leap beyond our body, our sensations, and all of our thoughts and emotions. And to make that leap, awareness has to familiarize itself with each of the centers and realize it is observing them.

The Intellectual Center

The intellectual center produces all mental constructs such as ideas, concepts, intellectual interests, logical comparisons, associative thoughts, and speculations. It is reading these words now, trying to comprehend or contradict these ideas, and probably relating them to other ideas it has heard or read about. The intellectual center responds to ideas and information with definitions, associations, opinions, and analytical opposition. It is the home of mental curiosity, inquisitiveness, and our sense of intelligence.

The intellectual center is also a storehouse for collecting, defining, sorting, and retrieving information. This is a useful instrument, yet despite its ability to give intellectual form to everything, it does not and cannot actually see anything. This sounds strange, but the fact is that the intellectual center *follows perception* and responds to what is seen by giving things a label, a name, a description, a meaning, or a cross-reference. When it cannot absorb something, it disallows, criticizes, and rejects it, be it ideas, people, opinions, situations, or events.

What is important to understand from the point of view of conscious awareness is that the intellectual center obscures being truly aware of—fully present to—whatever is right in front of us. Instead of awareness witnessing each remarkable moment that unfolds and absorbing it with unfiltered awareness, the intellectual center *displaces* awareness with associations, names, definitions, logical explanations, and memories.

Try, for instance, to walk or drive down the street and just look at what is in front of you as you go, without naming things or allowing tangential thoughts. If you succeed in simply being aware of being aware *of* what you see while sidestepping all thought *about* what you see, you will invariably discover the intellectual center trying to encroach on awareness with random thoughts and associations. You may even 'awaken' for a moment to the realization that awareness got so lulled by imagination in the intellectual center that you ceased, for a time, to see out of your eyes altogether.

The Emotional Center

The emotional center is the 'brain' that produces responses to people, to visual impressions, and to human events. These responses include feelings of like and dislike, judgment, envy, sentimentality, jealousy, patriotism, suspicion, criticism, sympathy, self-pity, anger, resentment, admiration, appreciation, compassion, and creative insight. The emotional center is especially sensitive to people and gets upset when it feels that other people do not pay us enough attention or give us enough respect. It is the root of our feeling of uniqueness and our sense of right. It is also the source of our approval and judgments of other people and ourselves. Inner-considering, which was described earlier, can start in the instinctive center but takes final shape in the emotional center.

Of all the lower centers, the emotional center is the fastest (the intellect is the slowest) and most perceptive when it is functioning properly. It has a capacity to appreciate nature, beauty, friendship, and the arts. It is sensitive to beauty and orderliness, be it a clean room, a flower arrangement, or a Greek statue. This same sensitivity can give rise to a deeper appreciation of the spectacle of life on earth and the fact that everything has come to exist in the first place. In this regard, the emotional center can bring us to the threshold of conscious awareness where we have the possibility of stepping beyond emotions and experiencing direct seeing—wordless beholding—from the perspective of pure awareness.

The Moving Center

The moving center is responsible for producing all physical movement, all sense of pleasure or inconvenience from movement, and all visualization of movement in space, such as when we drive a car or plan a project or play chess, or when we solve architectural, engineering, or programming problems. The moving center imitates, improvises, and invents, and it prides itself in its movements and physical accomplishments. It gets frustrated, too, when our momentum is interrupted by circumstances or by other people.

As the most visible of the four lower centers, the moving center is also the most mesmerizing. Movement gives us the appearance and feeling that we are conscious beings busy accomplishing things on planet earth. Often, the busier we are and the more we get done, the more alive and in control we seem to ourselves and to others. Yet, as the fourth way explains, movement is not an action of self-awareness or conscious will. It merely happens out of impulse *as a physical reaction.*

The moving center is so quick, so competent, and so consistent that it deceives its owner as well as other people into thinking that it is identity. What it cannot see, however, is how it automatically visualizes and anticipates each next movement so as to link all its movements into a smooth continuum. But, as in the intellectual and emotional centers, even useful functioning of the moving center tends to displace awareness of what is right in front of it. It moves nimbly *through* the moment without being consciously present *to* the moment and to what is *in* the moment.

Once we observe this, it is alarming to realize that we can go through a rapid series of elaborate movements—in the kitchen, at a desk, or behind the wheel of a car—without seeing clearly what is right in front of us. This realization can also be the beginning of a new understanding about what awareness is and what it implies.

The Instinctive Center

The fourth center in the human body is the instinctive center which *invisibly* governs the five senses and all the inner workings of our physical organism such as breathing, digestion, metabolism, sneezing, tissue building, and healing. Although most of these operations take place behind the scenes and undetected by the other three centers, the instinctive center is also the realm of sensations. For example, it is attuned to climate and temperature, to other people appearing sympathetic or threatening, and to the omnidirectional sense that we may be being watched or approached from behind.

The instinctive center also gives rise to intuitions such as sensing that a particular person may be in the vicinity, or that a relative may telephone soon. It can sometimes 'read' with uncanny accuracy the weaknesses or well being of others. And because all of these perceptions are wordless and invisible, they can deceive us into mistaking them for conscious awareness—when, in fact, the 'seeing' of conscious awareness has a very different origin, essence, and aspect.

Where the intellectual center logically explains what is in the moment, and where the emotional center evaluates and discriminates about what is in the moment, and where the moving center visualizes and manipulates the moment, the instinctive center senses and seizes upon the moment to ensure its welfare. With radarlike acuity, it stealthily notices, greedily clutches, selfishly hordes, and craftily takes advantage of the opportunity to gain, get ahead, and guard its survival.

More than any other center, the instinctive center exists for itself. It exhibits no interest in conscious awareness and is even opposed to it, largely because it believes that *it* is awareness, when in fact it is just a spectrum of keen sensations. Partly because of its keenness, however, its decision-making power governs the other lower centers and distracts awareness from being aware of being aware.

Fortunately, the trump card is held by conscious awareness which comes to realize that, although the instinctive center is keenly alert in its own right and aware of is own intensity, it cannot be aware of being aware. Only pure awareness can do that *and be that*.

Although we experience the world *through* our four centers, the experience is not conscious awareness. Conscious awareness watches the four centers and is aware of watching them.

The Connection Between Centers

While it is important to distinguish the four centers, it is equally important to understand how they are *connected* to each other. In brief, there are three main connections: between the intellectual and emotional center; between the emotional and moving center; and between the moving and instinctive center.

The strongest connection exists between the moving and instinctive center. In fact, it is so strong that they appear to act as one center in a bond that can be likened to a concrete wall (the moving center) and the rebar (instinctive center) that reinforces it. This powerful melding renders these two centers so integrated as to form a single unit that can, when needed, exist completely independently of the intellectual and emotional centers.

As Gurdjieff put it, the connection between our moving and instinctive centers can be thought of as a carriage and its wheels. Although they are separate, neither can exist in a practical way without the other. It also happens, not coincidentally, that they operate *at the same speed.*

Continuing Gurdjieff's analogy, the instinctive-moving 'carriage' is connected to the 'horse' of our emotional center by means of a harness and shaft. And although the emotional center could operate at a much *faster* speed than the moving and instinctive centers, it usually operates at their speed due to the harness that is designed to make the transfer of energy between them more smooth.

In this same analogy, a 'driver' holds the reigns and is responsible for guiding the horse and steering the carriage. This is the intellectual center which operates at a much *slower* speed than the trio of emotional, moving, and instinctive centers. But even though it is slower, the advantage is that it can regulate the other three centers. In effect, the driver can exercise reason, pull on the reigns, say "whoa" to the horse of emotions, and in turn bring the carriage under control or to a halt. As it turns out, this proves essential when it comes to controlling the expression of negative emotions.

As we will see later in this book, the creation of negative emotions typically begins as raw energy in the instinctive-moving centers (the carriage) before spilling into the emotional center (the horse) where it is embroidered as a personal feeling of 'I'. This feeling in turn percolates into the intellectual center where it is granted authenticity and given final permission to express itself (in a variety of ways) as a declaration of identity.

There is more to the formula behind how negative emotions form in our psyche and forge their way to expression, but the analogy of the carriage-horse-driver provides a vivid image of how the connections between the four centers contribute to negative emotions and to our sense of identity behind them.

It is also noteworthy that the intellectual and the moving-instinctive centers communicate to each other *through* the emotional center. This is noteworthy because although negative emotions originate in the moving and instinctive centers, and although they are rationalized in the intellectual center, it is in the emotional center that they substantiate our sense of self.

Meanwhile, unbeknownst to the carriage, the horse, and often the driver, there is a silent, unseen passenger inside the carriage. If our four centers were properly aligned and connected, this 'passenger' of awareness would govern our life: it would consciously prompt the driver to guide the horse and steer the carriage. In other words, we would live out life from the top down. But as it is, the process happens in reverse from the bottom up: the carriage unwittingly pulls the horse; the horse drags the driver along; and the passenger remains 'asleep' in the back seat.

According to the fourth way, the remedy to all this is twofold. First and foremost, the passenger needs to recognize itself, realize itself, actualize itself: awareness has to become aware of being aware, which is what self-remembering is about. At the same time, the four centers need to be aligned and balanced so they can support and respond to conscious awareness, which is what the non-expression of negative emotions is about.

Non-expression is powerful because it exposes and weakens the sense of 'I' we experience in the four centers. In parallel, self-remembering renders awareness aware of being conscious. Both the seer and the seen become more apparent, which is the crux of spiritual awakening and enlightenment.

'Obstacles' to Awareness

It was mentioned earlier that awareness is generally elusive because of certain tendencies in our psychology. Namely, identification, imagination, inner-considering, and the expression of negative emotions. Sometimes these are referred to in the fourth way as obstacles that must be overcome or as barriers that must be broken through, and that special 'effort' is required to achieve this. It is important to understand, however, what the word effort means in this context.

One way to understand it is in terms of the connections between centers. For example, if you look closely at identification, imagination, inner-considering, and not just the expression of negative emotions but how negative emotions form, you will discover that all these tendencies are a consequence of one or more weak connections between the centers.

When the four centers are properly aligned and balanced, and when the connections between them are sufficiently strong, many psychological 'tendencies' would not exist, or would at least be greatly minimized, and self-remembering (awareness aware of being aware) could establish *and* maintain itself more effectively.

In this context, 'effort' means not so much doing things as not doing things so that awareness can be effortlessly aware of being aware at all times.

Essence and Personality

For the purposes of self-study, the fourth way also distinguishes two other aspects of our being which are called essence and personality. Essence refers to who and what we are as we are born, including our physical constitution (race, culture, temperament, magnetism), our psychological makeup (the way we interpret and respond to the world), and our natural propensities (athleticism, artistic talent, academic interests, intuitive know-how). None of these are learned or borrowed or contrived. They are inherent at birth and although they may be camouflaged or suppressed during our life, they never change.

By contrast, personality is not inherent. It is everything we learn, everything we are taught, everything we imitate, everything we *try to become*. It is the mask—the persona—we wear during our earthly life. This mask changes expressions and even tone of voice when circumstances change. For instance, we wear one mask at the office, another at home, another when things are going well, and another when we are under pressure. The differences in our masks can be dramatic or subtle depending on our psychological mood and the circumstances at hand. The differences can also be hard to detect because of the underlying feeling of 'me' that supports them.

Whereas personality is reactive, essence is receptive and easily affected by things like nature and beauty as well as by industry, brutality, changes in the weather, and cycles of the moon and planets. Personality also serves shields and minimizes the effect of certain influences and, in right order, protects and orients essence. What often happens, however, is that personality takes on a life of its own and we start—generally at an early age—to believe that we are our personality, its shield, and its masks. As a consequence, we lose touch with our simple, true nature of essence.

Conscious Transformation

Although personality has an important purpose in our human makeup, it stems from a false sense of identity that *imagines* itself inwardly and *projects* itself outwardly. And one of the most corrupting aspects of personality is how it learns to manufacture, indulge in, and express negative emotions. This is harmful because, as described earlier, negative emotions negate essence's ability to see with clear awareness.

Essence is also more than our human nature. At its core it is an expression of simple, pure, unadulterated awareness. But it is not conscious of itself. It is not *aware of being aware.*

By not expressing negative emotions *and* understanding the purpose of not expressing them, we start to free essence from the grip of personality. This in turn enables the awareness of essence to transform itself beyond the realm of thought (beyond the 'driver' of the intellect) in a way that cannot be described in words.

The Ray of Creation

It is enormous to realize the significance of simple awareness and how negative emotions impede awareness. But to fully comprehend both of these, we have to connect them to our existence within the context of the solar system, the galaxy, and the universe.

The fourth way explains this larger context as the 'Ray of Creation'. The main principle of this idea is that the universe operates as a single whole and that *everything* is connected to and has a prescribed purpose in the whole. This includes existence as human beings on earth *and* the potential of awareness to consciously realize itself.

According to the fourth way, the Ray of Creation encompasses our known universe and extends all the way to the earth and, last but not least, to the moon. The Ray begins at the 'Absolute' which spawns the 'world' of all galaxies, which in turn spawn the world of all suns in all galaxies. All suns then spawn the world of all planets which includes—in our branch of the ray—our solar system and the earth, which in turn is spawning the moon.

In this scheme, higher worlds transmit influences to lower worlds which receive those influences, add their own, and continue the transmission down the ray. Each lower world is nested inside the worlds above it.

As human beings, we find ourselves as part of the thin film of 'organic life' on the earth's surface. This film comprises the earth's atmosphere and oceans as well as the human, animal, vegetable, and mineral kingdoms. All these together encase the earth like a sheath that filters and transmits celestial influences. This sheath also plays a special role by virtue of residing between the planets and the earth *and* between the earth and moon.

The fourth way explains that organic life is a special contrivance designed to ensure the transmission of influences from planets to earth and from earth to moon, and that mankind plays a special role in this contrivance. Each of us, by means of our physical, psychological, and metaphysical nature, acts as a tiny 'antenna' that receives 'influences' from higher worlds. Invidually and collectively, we receive influences from the sun and planets and transmit them to the earth and moon.

We are unwittingly locked into this arrangement. *Everything* about our lives is driven by it. But we don't notice this because the Ray of Creation is inconceivably large and we are infinitesimally small, *and* because awareness is usually restricted to the minutia of our personal lives. We barely see ourselves as part of a community or city—or at best a country. And the idea of a global village is, for most people, little more than a concept or ideal.

Beyond that, we usually regard animals, plants, nature, and the rest of organic life as something we are separate from, not part of and connected to. The solar system and galaxies are 'out there' and have no real relevance to us. Rarely do we comprehend anything about our existence *inside* those higher worlds as part of an all-encompassing 'Absolute' where everything is one.

Our existence in the Ray of Creation takes on particular meaning in terms of the psychological tendencies that obstruct awareness. This is because the intricate machinery of our psychology plays a key role in the way we receive and transmit influences coming from the Ray of Creation—which we do by means of imagination, identification, and negative emotions. All of these psychological mechanisms conduct influences to the earth and to the moon, yet we usually interpret their *effect* as our own: as 'my' appearance, my impulses, my skills, my thoughts, my emotions, my decisions, and my behavior. When higher influences act on us, they also act through us by vivifying a sense of identity which *camouflages* the fact that we are mere conduits within the enormous interchange of influences taking place between sun-planets-earth-moon.

This interchange occurs mainly via identification and negative emotions. Imagination and identification form the conduit and negative emotions provide the current passing through it. The deeper our imagination and the stronger our identification, the more we reinforce the conduit and the more we convert the rarefied material of awareness into the voltage of negative emotions which shuffles through us as an urgent sense of 'me'.

Negative emotions may seem inconsequential on an individual basis, but when you multiply their effect by eight billion humans, the impact on a planetary scale is palpable. Suffice it to say that humanity and the earth would be very different without human beings manufacturing, indulging in, and expressing negative emotions. At the same time, however, this would not benefit the larger purposes of the Ray of Creation. It would benefit *only individuals.*

For those individuals, the benefit comes in two forms: it loosens the grip that negative emotions have over awareness, and it severs the cable of identification that keeps awareness tied to the earth and tethered to the moon.

From this perspective, being more conscious about not identifying with negative emotions inwardly and not expressing them outwardly signals a profound turnaround in our psychology that points to the realization of awareness itself and the possibility of transforming this finest energy of which we are composed.

The Nature of Negative Emotions

The emotional center borrows material from the instinctive center, and with the negative half of the instinctive center and the help of imagination and identification, it creates negative emotions.
Peter Ouspensky

NEGATIVE EMOTIONS are usually the first place we go when we encounter discomfort, inconvenience, and suffering. Such is the nature of psychological 'sleep' to immediately *shield ourselves* against the forces that can awaken us.

Negative emotions are a reaction, not a perception. In this sense, they are not really emotions. They are defense mechanisms that prevent the possibility of full emotion.

With negative emotions, we turn away from what is really happening. We dig a hole and bury our awareness in it. Conquering a negative emotion means uncovering the hole. Transformation means releasing conscious awareness back into the open air.

Negative emotions have us see the world in relation to ourselves instead of ourselves in relation to a much, much larger world and the laws governing it. We don't usually see the world. We respond to it and see *that*.

Negative emotions represent our disagreement with reality, which is ridiculous when you think about it.

Negative emotions are harmful not so much for what they are, but because they steal our ability to control our consciousness of awareness. Recapturing this ability is what transformation and spiritual evolution are all about.

Negative emotions reinforce our imaginary feeling of 'I'. Starving negative emotions (by not expressing them) and dismantling them (by neutralizing the faulty thinking that allows them) causes our familiar sense of 'me' to fall apart and be exposed as the fragmented thing that it is.

Negative emotions lie at the hub of imaginary 'I'. They connect the spokes of our myriad thoughts, feelings, and behavior that keep awareness asleep. This is why work on negative emotions is so pivotal.

Negative emotions are a psychological spider web. They trap awareness.

Awareness falls asleep in negative emotions. But even when we begin to know this, awareness cannot collect itself because the pull of negativity is stronger than the will of conscious awareness. This shows us what we are up against and how elusive awareness is.

Influences come from outside, we respond to them with an interpretation of negative emotions, and we express negative emotions to protect our imaginary sense of 'I'.

It is naive to think that expressing negative emotions is harmless or meaningless. It is a mechanical link in a large mechanical chain. We just don't see the chain.

Negative emotions are strings that make us puppets. Stopping their expression is a way to resist the pull of the puppeteer, but we are still attached. It takes transformation to cut the strings.

Negative emotions are the result of awareness being corrupted by unpleasant sensations in the instinctive center and by negative attitudes in the intellectual center—both of which spill into the emotional center and corrupt it.

Where there is negativity, there are psychological blinders which the system calls buffers. These buffers lurk behind the instinctive center and our imaginary picture (feeling) of 'I' and camouflage them.

Because we are not consciously aware, we do not perceive things directly. Instead, we receive them through attitudes. To free perception and make it more conscious, we have to unlock our attitudes, especially our negative attitudes.

We are simply trying to see things as they are. Negative emotions prevent this by keeping awareness prisoner in a distorted form of perception and thought.

When we take negative emotions away, we start to see the smallness and emptiness of our emotional existence as human beings on the earth.

What the system calls the 'machine' (our body and multiple feelings of 'I') is the prison. Negative emotions are the lock on the door. The aim is to open the lock so conscious awareness can go free.

It helps to know precisely what a negative emotion is based on: both the subject and the source within. The 'blame' does not lie outside.

A grudge is a type of negative emotion that psychologically shuts the door on other people to punish them for offending our imaginary picture of ourselves. In actuality, though, grudges shut awareness further inside the cocoon of our imaginary sense of 'I'. It is a bizarre kind of defense mechanism.

Grudges are one way to see that negative emotions are the place where we are the most asleep in our illusion of 'I', and how hard it is for awareness to step out of this illusion and stay free from it.

From one point of view, negative emotions don't really exist. They are like a hologram that appears real but which vanishes when you see it from the correct angle—or, in our case, from the perspective of awareness.

It is strange that awareness, which is real, is held in check by negative emotions, which are artificial and unnecessary. Even stranger is how much we believe negative emotions and that we have to train ourselves not to believe them.

A common trait of negative emotions is the feeling of 'no', of negation. The same thing exists in the thinking behind negative emotions. Something is being denied. It feels justified, yet it is backwards from reality. We are what has to change.

To conquer negative emotions is to conquer our imaginary picture of 'I'. Negative emotions hide the fact that this imaginary picture is imaginary.

Negative emotions represent one of the strongest forces if not *the* strongest force in human psychology. If we can neutralize this force, we can unlatch the hold that the many 'I's have over awareness.

If negative emotions did not exist, there would be little psychology to study. 'Identity' would collapse and become very simple.

When we see ourselves expressing negative emotions, we are seeing a reflection of the false picture we imagine ourselves to be. What sees this is awareness, but only for a fraction of a second because untrained awareness is immediately dimmed or shut off when negative emotions are expressed.

When someone else expresses negative emotions, watch carefully and you will see that the energy behind the expression has its roots in the person's instinctive center, like a viper. The rest, as Mr. Ouspensky said, is "emotional embroidery" that is fashioned by false personality. We can see the same thing in ourselves.

Negative emotions are not isolated psychological events, and they are not as personal as they seem. They have another purpose which is connected to man's role in organic life on earth as a receiver and transmitter of influences that pass between the sun, the earth, and the moon. As long as awareness remains identified with negative emotions, it remains plugged into this circuit. To 'unplug' is a tremendous change that brings an inner transformation of awareness.

As human beings within the thin film of 'organic life' on the surface of the earth, we receive and transmit planetary influences that no other form of life is capable of doing. For example, the atmosphere, the oceans, the animal kingdom, and the vegetable kingdom do not manufacture, indulge in, or express negative *emotions*. The human apparatus is specifically designed to do this, not for its own sake but for the purposes of organic life and its function in the Ray of Creation.

The atmosphere, the oceans, the animal kingdom, and the vegetable kingdom also do not possess man's capacity for conscious awareness. This, too, is part of the design of human beings which are tiny, complex, highly sensitive components in a bigger scheme.

The silver lining is that whereas negative emotions are necessary for the collective purposes of organic life, they are not necessary for us individually. Awareness *can* unplug, *can* escape, *can* slip out unnoticed by the larger laws of the universe, and this is not a random possibility. It, too, is accounted for in the design of organic life.

Awareness is nimble and light. By contrast, negative emotions are a crude hardening of perception. Indulging in and expressing them is akin to awareness stepping into quicksand and disappearing.

Peter Ouspensky said that the raw material for negative emotions is "borrowed" from the instinctive center and fabricated into negative emotions by negative imagination and identification. One area where this is evident is between couples. Nearly all the tension, irritation, frustration, disagreement, resentment, anger, and gossip that couples engage in toward each other is instinctive in origin and then becomes emotional. This also points to something else Mr. Ouspensky said: that as long as we cannot control the expression of negative emotions, we cannot control anything else with regard to the instinctive center. Only when we can control non-expression can we have command over the raw material behind negative emotions. It is like having to break a wild horse before we can ride it.

Impressions of all kinds are constantly available to us but they cannot be digested, much less transformed, because our instrument for receiving and processing them doesn't work as it should. In this sense, the expression of negative emotions could be called the "expulsion of higher matter" that we cannot absorb.

This changes when awareness is consciously aware. Impressions then enter unimpeded and find their proper place in perception. At the same time, negative emotions lose their zeal and power of resistance, and start to become an unnecessary part of our being.

The Role of Non-Expression

If you choose, you are free. If you choose,
you need blame no man, accuse no man.
Epictetus

NEGATIVE EMOTIONS negate, deny, reject, and resist reality. Controlling the expression of negative emotions throws light on this fact.

The non-expression of negative emotions stifles the instinctive center and interrupts the logic of imaginary 'I'. It highlights what awareness *is not.*

Not expressing negative emotions is a way to reclaim the internal space that rightfully belongs to impartial awareness.

We—as awareness—are usually caught *inside* a negative emotion. Not-expressing it is the first step to getting outside it.

Not expressing negative emotions creates psychological pressure, but this pressure is helpful and in no way harmful because *used correctly* it enables us to see how binding negative emotions are.

Not expressing negative emotions is the practical basis of psychological thinking—thinking which is geared toward conscious awareness.

The external world acts as a stimulus or first force. 'I's and attitudes, many of them rooted in the negative halves of centers, act as second force that reacts and responds to the stimulus. Identification (the psychological condition of 'losing oneself' in something) is the third force that makes it possible for the first two forces to merge and form negative emotions. Not expressing negative emotions uncouples this triad by dissolving the psychological process of identification, which in turn leads to a more conscious state of awareness. Instead of *being* the negative emotion, awareness *sees* the negative emotion and is aware of seeing it.

Not expressing negative emotions can become a way of prolonging conscious awareness.

The expression of negative emotions reinforces our feeling of "I am negative" or "I am hurt." Non-expression exposes this feeling of 'I' and shows how it is rooted in our imaginary picture of self.

Negative attitudes and negative emotions push awareness down. Adjusting our attitudes and reducing our degree of identification with the 'problem' lift awareness up and out.

The mechanism of expressing negative emotions is like a ceiling fan that draws in surrounding air and pushes it downward. In effect, negative emotions hurl the material of awareness into a lower, more dense form. Non-expression slows this downward spiral and can bring it to a halt. We can then find the small switch in ourselves which makes the fan spin in the opposite direction, upward. But there is a period, a pause, when awareness is moving neither up nor down. At first, it feels like emptiness. This is the "stillness of non-expression" which precedes the transformation and transmutation of awareness as conscious awareness.

Indulging in and expressing negative emotions confines awareness. Not expressing them releases it. More accurately, it allows awareness to release itself.

The periodic non-expression of negative emotions does not produce transformation. It can interrupt one negative emotion, but another one can lure awareness in again because the observer in us is still more identified than it is conscious. It has enough observation but not enough conscious awareness to keep itself independent of the negative emotions it observes. This observer has to find a way to *let go* of what it is observing.

When matter is compressed, it generates heat and energy. This is what happens in a car engine, in a hurricane, and in the non-expression of negative emotions. In our case, the purpose of non-expression and non-identification is to force the 'molecules' of negativity inward and upward so they can be consciously distilled.

We are not interested in negative emotions themselves, but in the fuel they burn. By not expressing negative emotions, we contain this energy. The more consciously we contain it, the more we extract and use it for conscious awareness.

Not expressing negative emotions is an attempt to escape from the mechanical unity of imaginary 'I'. Transformation is an attempt to promote the conscious unity of awareness.

Not expressing a negative emotion does not mean suppressing it. As Mr. Ouspensky said, when we suppress we keep the identification, whereas the purpose of not expressing is to promote non-identification.

True non-expression means that awareness leaves the negative emotion alone and distances itself as a pure observer. The negative emotion remains *inside* but awareness withdraws its identification. This dissolves the negative emotion, sometimes immediately, sometimes longer, depending on the intensity.

Negative emotions simply cannot survive without identification—without the immersion and collusion of awareness. Without this component as catalyst, negative emotions fall apart, dissolve, disappear—which brings relief, lightness, and energy to awareness.

By the time we are on the verge of expressing a negative emotion, a lot has already happened in our inner world. The negative emotion has sprouted, established itself, gained momentum, and is ready to burst. At this point, it takes considerable conscious effort to *not allow it* to be expressed. This is also just the beginning. We then have to work backwards, look at the negativity, determine how the particular negative emotion formed itself, and tunnel to its root in our false sense of 'I'".

Once a negative emotion is expressed, most of the material we need for observation is gone. Expressing it has burned the energy that awareness needs to be aware. Once we really understand this, the non-expression of negative emotions takes on new meaning and value.

Expressing negative emotions exhausts fine energy, scatters it, and petrifies *the potential* of awareness. Not expressing negative emotions starts to contain that energy and distill awareness from it.

To be aware of being aware of negative emotions is the real meaning of "separating the fine from the coarse." Transformation leads to a process of keeping the fine and disposing the coarse.

Non-expression and non-identification represent successive notes in the ascending octave of transformation.

Identification and non-identification both have degrees.

Not expressing negative emotions already requires a degree of non-identification.

The mass of our negative emotions forms a thick barricade that prevents awareness from returning to its place of origin.

The non-expression of negative emotions is a lever.

Non-expression is a tool for awareness to distinguish between itself and negative 'I's. Non-identification is a process of consciously detaching from the sense of self underlying the 'I's.

There is a direct relationship between negative emotions and our imaginary picture of 'me'. Not expressing negative emotions reveals this connection and starts to loosen it so that awareness can slip free and consciously realize itself.

Negative Emotions and Denying Force

Suffering becomes deliberate if you don't rebel against it, if you don't try to avoid it, if you don't accuse anybody, if you accept it as a necessary part of your work at the moment and as a means for attaining your aim.
Peter Ouspensky

IN THE SYSTEM, 'denying force' refers to all forms of discomfort, unpleasantness, inconvenience, interruption, misfortune, pain, and tragedy which cause friction and suffering in our life, which in turn usually result in some kind of negative emotion followed by its outward expression.

Friction and suffering create internal pressure which we don't know how to accommodate, so we psychologically process that pressure through the internal mechanism of negative emotions and then expel it through physical expression. In short, negative emotions serve as a conduit and relief valve for the pressure *and the material* of denying force.

We are taught almost from birth to have a negative attitude toward denying force: to dislike it, see it as a hindrance or problem, and want to avoid it.

Viewing denying force with a neutral attitude requires self-remembering: the self of awareness 'remembering' to be consciously aware in the face of friction and regarding it's pressure as a catalyst.

Most negative emotions originate in the instinctive center (the center of sensations) because the instinctive center is designed to *resist the discomfort* caused by denying force.

Changing our attitude about denying force changes our relationship to negative emotions. Instead of denying force seeming inappropriate and wrong and negative emotions feeling justified and right, denying force starts to have new meaning and negative emotions start to be seen as blinders of avoidance.

Denying force brings our imaginary sense of 'I' out of hiding. This deeper sense of 'I' gets negative when it cannot do things or have things its way. Because it doesn't like friction, it pops to the surface and expresses negativity whenever denying force appears—which is one of the best times to see and realize this false sense of 'me', and to begin the internal separation between it and awareness of it.

The secret behind the friction caused by denying force is that its intensified energy can help awareness realize itself 'above' negative emotions as the conscious observer of them.

A lot of negative emotions stem from the illusion that we should be afraid of denying force. We are surprisingly reluctant to give up this illusion because it means giving up the illusion of 'I'.

A subtle aspect of human nature that keeps awareness in check (asleep) is the impulse to protect ourselves *and others* from denying force. Our imaginary sense of 'I' doesn't want to see beyond other people's imaginary sense of 'I' either.

Imaginary 'I' or ego, which takes different forms in different people, is prone to expectations. Expectations give our imaginary 'I' *permission* to become negative when its expectations are not met.

A negative attitude toward denying force prevents transformation because it thwarts separation, not just the separation of awareness from denying force, but from our *reaction to* denying force. This reaction is also a denying force, an internal one.

There are no external obstacles to the awakening of awareness and all of the internal ones are imaginary. It is wonderful to realize this and hard to remember it.

An accepting attitude toward friction does not make the friction lighter. It makes awareness lighter and more conscious.

The negative halves of centers produce negative thoughts, feelings, postures, and sensations which drag awareness down. Positive halves of centers help make awareness lighter, faster, freer.

The popular notion of positive thinking is a buffer and an end in itself rather than a means to conscious awareness. True positive emotion does not mean being more 'positive'. It means being more aware of what is going on in front of us and inside us without awareness being governed by it (identified with it).

Accepting denying force is a way to move out of the negative halves of centers into the positive halves, not for its own sake but to promote conscious awareness.

Denying force seems grueling because we identify with it (lose awareness in it). Denying force itself is often simple and short-lived, but imaginary 'I' complicates it with identification as a way of prolonging the sense of 'me' confronted with denying force.

It is useful to examine why we dislike a particular denying force. It is usually some kind of avoidance in imaginary 'I' or resistance in the instinctive center, or both. These parts of ourselves don't want to face the reality of what is happening. Nor do they understand what is possible in terms of awareness.

Friction and suffering usually consume the substance of awareness, yet those same catalysts make possible the awakening of conscious awareness.

Logical thinking means viewing things in terms of their opposite: good and bad, right and wrong, yes or no. Psychological thinking means viewing things in terms of how they are connected, such as how friction is connected to the possibility of promoting consciousness.

Logical thinking about denying force freezes awareness and holds it in check. Psychological thinking about denying force unlocks awareness and springs it free.

Psychological thinking rises above negative imagination and looks at friction in the context of *using it* to arouse and heighten awareness. This minimizes identification and fosters conscious awareness.

We garner an imaginary identity through resistance to friction and set ourselves up to become negative about denying force.

We cannot transcend suffering until we move past the negative emotions that avoid and blame and feel sorry about *and try to resist* the suffering. Negative emotions are a veil we have to lift to reach transformation.

Denying force is simply a producer of the raw material of friction. Friction, in turn, is a producer of energy that generates the light of conscious awareness.

Denying force is associated with the 'passive' force in a triad, yet no force in a triad is passive in the sense of being inert or inactive. Every force is active; it is simply that its inner dynamic varies according to its place—its function—in the triad.

Negative emotions can occupy different places in a triad. Expressing them means one place in a triad. Non-expression puts them in another place. And transformation in slightly another.

Denying force is not the 'obstacle' it appears to be to our four lower centers. Rather, it is a conductor of material and energy. The question is whether this material provokes in us an automatic response of physical and psychological resistance, or whether it can be appropriated as part of a conscious triad.

Peter Ouspensky explained that energy is the mechanical side of consciousness, just as the sun's heat is the mechanical side of its light. In the same way, awareness needs fuel to give it ignition. The energy *behind* negative emotions is one such fuel—one of the most potent at our disposal.

Conscious awareness remains independent of the fuel that fires it.

The Process of Transformation

When the fire is strong, it soon appropriates
to itself the matter which is heaped on it,
and consumes it, and rises higher by means
of this very material.
Marcus Aurelius

THE NON-EXPRESSION of negative emotions is not enough by itself because it is primarily an effort by the mind to harness attention. This effort needs to be complemented with conscious awareness—pure awareness aware of being aware.

Non-identification means awareness being consciously aware of itself independent from the struggle that is taking place between negative emotions and the effort not to express them.

Transformation is *based* on non-expression and *depends* on non-identification.

Not expressing negative emotions creates internal pressure. The more this pressure can be sustained, the more it pulls things apart, like water that keeps boiling until its lighter molecules break free as pure air—pure aw-air-ness.

Not expressing negative emotions represents control over our lower centers (of sensations, movements, thoughts, and emotions) whereas non-identification represents awareness controlling itself and being aware of doing so.

Transformation leads to a state of non-identification that is aware of being aware. The observer transforms itself into a conscious observer.

We cannot fully describe the work of non-identification because it is beyond the lower centers and therefore beyond words.

Negative emotions are noisy. Transformation is silent.

Transformation cannot occur in our ordinary state of consciousness because we are still *inside* the negative emotion or suffering. We first have to get outside, which is the purpose of acceptance, non-expression, and non-identification. Transformation begins when awareness *knowingly* gets outside a negative emotion.

Even in our best attempts to use right attitudes for transformation, we eventually have to jump to another scale. Awareness has to harness attitudes as a springboard to a higher level of conscious awareness.

Transformation occurs above whatever is being transformed. We don't turn something into something else so much as something higher recognizes itself above something lower and is no longer trapped in the negative emotion or suffering.

Awareness becomes conscious of itself above negative emotions. Above everything.

Awareness is what gets transformed. The thing supposedly being transformed is still there, but it gets left behind. It falls away like a booster rocket.

Instead of us expressing anger about a negative situation or event, we can view it as a catalyst, as a stepping stone for the delicate presence of awareness to come into conscious being. Internally, some 'I's will still storm down a path of negativity, but awareness chooses not to go along. It takes the high road and transforms the event into pure awareness of it.

Lower states of consciousness exist inside the lower centers, inside the physical and psychological world of 'I's. Higher states occur outside the 'I's in higher centers as a state of awareness that is aware of being aware.

A generator converts mechanical energy into electrical energy. This is what the mind does when it converts the thinking behind negative emotions into useful attitudes. A re-generator, on the other hand, implies something else working on the electrical energy and using *that*, converting it yet again. The remote witness of awareness fully separate, aware, and watching.

A generator converts energy. A transformer boosts it.

Negative emotions vary, but the experience of transforming and transcending them remains the same.

Transformation is neither the attitudes leading to it nor the emotions resulting from it. It is a calm, wordless state of detached awareness.

Negative emotions are so fast. Conscious awareness is the only thing that can stay ahead of negative emotions and *already be there* when they arrive.

The more we can see negative emotions, the better, because this means that the observer of awareness is separate from them and seeing them. The observer just needs to learn to keep its distance and stay aware.

Transformation remains elusive even when we think we know how to do it. This is because *knowing how* to do it is a trace of understanding in the mind whereas *actually doing* it is an experience of awareness.

Although the mind cannot command the consciousness of awareness, it can summon the memory of what pure awareness feels like, just as we can summon the memory of what chocolate tastes like. This 'recall' can bring us to, or closer to, the pure presence of conscious awareness.

The job of the intellect is not to reach awareness, but to prompt awareness so that transformation can occur.

Transforming Negative Emotions

Negative emotions negate our position in relation to the larger whole, and in doing so they negate the whole. No awareness exists except 'me'. Everything else is shut out. Positive emotions, on the other hand, come as a result of seeing the whole and our place in it. Everything exists. Nothing is shut out. Awareness is purified and clear.

The word positive derives from 'posit' which means to place, and the word universe derives from 'unus' (one) and 'versum' (to turn). In other words, everything revolves around a central whole, has its place in relation to the whole, and through awareness can combine with the whole. Conscious awareness perceives this and its perception yields positive emotions. The mind can also understand this well enough to reconstruct a point of view that can turn negation into acceptance, acceptance into seeing, and seeing into conscious awareness.

Each negative emotion is like a psychological glove we are trying to turn inside-out. We do this by recognizing that the source and cause of all negativity is inside ourselves and in our attitudes, not in a person or thing or event. The more we master this understanding, the faster we are able to turn a negative emotion around and use it for conscious awareness.

Each negative emotion is like a loaf of bread made from the ingredients of instinctive energy, negative imagination, and the attitudes of imaginary 'I'. The yeast that enables this loaf to rise is identification. What we are trying to learn is how not to add the yeast, how to unmix the ingredients, and how to extract conscious food from them.

Just as a person can be aware of himself looking at a tree, awareness can be aware of itself looking at a negative emotion. In both cases, the role of the object being viewed is to reflect the observer *back to itself* and help the observer become aware of itself as the observer.

If we can see how we become identified, we can see how to become un-identified, and how not to become identified. In other words, we can find our way to being consciously aware.

The mind understands this and tries to enact it, but it cannot be it because non-identification is not a quality of the mind, but of awareness.

Beyond the reach of all the 'I's there is an empty place—the "quiet place within" that Mr. Ouspensky speaks of. This is where transformation occurs. The 'I's cannot get there. Only pure awareness resides there.

The whole thing is about awareness learning not to be identified—learning not to derive identity from what it perceives internally or externally. As Nisargadatta said, "The world is made of rings. The hooks are all yours. Unbend your hooks."

Non-identification invalidates negative emotions. It strips them of identity.

Identification is like a cable that the current of negative emotions pass through. Its purpose is to transmit negatively charged energy to the earth and moon. Cutting this cable in ourselves is a significant event not just on the scale of human life, but on the scale of organic life, the earth, the moon, the planets, the sun, and higher.

Properly containing the outer expression of a negative emotion 'lifts' awareness even as the negative emotion continues to flail about internally.

As awareness steps away from a negative emotion internally, it finds itself in new territory. The inner world—the "kingdom within"—starts to open up, expand, and reveal new depth. This is the beginning of transformation and non-expression unlocks the door to it .

Ideally, awareness is already present before a negative emotion starts to form, in which case the emotion never builds enough momentum to reach the point of expression. Usually, however, it happens the other way around because awareness is absent. In that case, a negative emotion takes shape, justifies itself, urges to express itself, and that urge nudges awareness enough for us to put a lid on the expression. We then find ourselves working backwards from the expression to the root cause and our identification with it. It's like walking backwards through the maze of our psychology. Until, that is, awareness realizes the whole thing has to do with identification and learns intuitively to 'drop' identification and just jump into itself as awareness.

As Mr. Ouspensky pointed out, there are two main stages of identification: one where we are becoming identified, and one where identification is complete. The same is true about negative emotions. In both cases, transformation is about awareness being conscious before the process completes itself, and eventually being there as—or before—it starts.

The fourth way states that as humans we need three types of sustenance to survive: food, air, and impressions. The most important of these is impressions, which is no accident when you consider that the strongest impressions we see come to us via reflections of light and that awareness itself is essentially light.

There is another type of sustenance but it is intended for higher centers and higher realms of awareness. This other sustenance comes through the friction and suffering that are produced by our encounters with denying force. The 'rubbing' brought about by denying force produce a spark. This spark can either ignite negative emotions and create an 'explosion' through expression, or it can promote a transformation of conscious awareness.

Negative emotions serve as 'buffers' that deflect friction and suffering. They push back on denying force and regurgitate the 'food' of friction because they cannot digest this material. It is not an exaggeration to say that expressing negative emotions is akin to spitting out material we cannot consciously digest.

The higher centers of awareness, however, can digest and transform this material. The spark caused by friction can give awareness 'lift'. Not expressing negative emotions is simply a way of containing the spark long enough for it to ignite and propel conscious awareness.

When you consider how many human beings on earth react to friction and suffering with negative emotions and then respond with the expression of negative emotions, it paints a powerful picture of the role that humanity plays in organic life on earth as a receiver and re-transmitter of energy in the solar system. When you compare this to awareness consciously absorbing friction, it paints an even more powerful picture of what is possible through non-expression and transformation.

The human expression of negative emotions plays a special role in organic life. In sync with the moon—like interlocking wheels in a clock, one small and one large—it ensures the transmission of planetary 'influences'. But once awareness consciously establishes itself, negative emotions start to fall away, just as organic life may start to fall away once the moon establishes its own rotation and self-sustaining magnetism.

At the root of negative emotions and their expression is what the fourth way calls chief feature, which is the hub of our imaginary 'I', the mental picture and emotional feeling of who we imagine we are. Chief feature is the psychological axis that drives imaginary 'I' and awareness is usually embedded in this picture as a result of identification. Stepping outside this psychological framework is difficult for awareness to do, and that is where the non-expression of negative emotions comes in.

By stifling the release of negative emotions, non-expression renders negative emotions, their expression, their construction, and their source visible to awareness. In the process, it enables awareness to distance itself internally from what it sees and recognize itself as the seer of negative emotions. The more this happens, the more imaginary 'I' dissolves and the more awareness transforms as conscious awareness.

The expression of negative emotions and everything leading to it is part of a descending octave that transmits influences *down* the Ray of Creation. Meanwhile, non-expression and non-identification are part of an ascending octave that reflects back *up* the Ray of Creation—*to its origin.*

Transformation and Awareness

All below duly travel'd, and still I mount
and mount. Rise after rise bow the
phantoms behind me.
Walt Whitman

BECAUSE AWARENESS IS not consciously aware, we simply forget about transformation. A negative emotion comes, we forget, and we express it.

Even when we try not to express a negative emotion, the possibility of transformation can get overwhelmed by self-doubt. The negativity seems too powerful and real, and transformation seems beyond our ability. We have to transcend these attitudes, too.

We have to see friction, denying force, suffering, and negative emotions as stepping stones instead of stumbling blocks.

'I's from the instinctive center and imaginary 'I' want to keep awareness involved in the struggle with negative emotions. They *want* awareness to fight on their level and on their terms, which means identification. That way, they keep awareness focused on negative emotions instead of on itself. Awareness has to learn to shift its focus and play the game at a higher level *above the struggle.*

One reason transformation is difficult is that the emotional center is entangled in the instinctive center. When something happens to irritate the instinctive center, its reaction prompts a parallel reaction in the emotional center. Conscious awareness is required to keep the emotional center out of the instinctive center's reactions, and to pull it out when the instinctive center tries to pull it in. It is exactly this overlap, brought about by identification, which prevents transformation.

For negative emotions to be transformed, they have to be brought to the surface and be exposed. In the discomfort of this process, we confront our imaginary picture of 'I' because seeing that is part of the experience of transforming the Self of awareness that sees it. But even when we start to see it, we become identified with it in the form of dismay or self-judgment or hopelessness. Awareness has to stay afloat above those waves, too.

If we are honest, we see that we are preoccupied with our own life. It is an ongoing subject of speculation, worry, and selfish manipulation. Usually we don't realize that this is all sleep and that what we call 'my life' is really material for something else.

We finally become negative about our inability to transform negative emotions and realize we have to start there.

The self of awareness is *never* negative. It just seems that way to the 'I's because all they know is imaginary 'I'.

The human mind is clever. It will control the outward expression of negativity to an extent and declare victory while still indulging negative 'I's inwardly. Even when we cut off the head of the worm that wants to express itself, the tail keeps wiggling. We then have to find a deeper level of non-expression and non-identification. Awareness has to isolate itself further, and then even further.

The mind and its emotions are not transformation. They are the platform. The wordless observer of awareness needs to see this and learn to 'ride' emotions.

One pitfall is to try too hard *mentally* to do this work, instead of using the mind as a jumping off point. Ultimately, 'work' means conscious awareness *being* itself.

We may successfully separate from negative 'I's, yet still fall prey to a deeper underlying mood that is harder to drop. It then becomes clear that the only thing which slips through the net of transformation is pure awareness.

Mr. Ouspensky spoke about "not being afraid to take the second step." A simple example of this is to act (pretend to be) less—even just a little less—negative than we feel. Sometimes 'acting' gives awareness enough space internally to establish control over itself.

Negative emotions are small but seem big because our imaginary sense of 'I' is afraid of being insignificant, being seen as insignificant, and being left behind.

One of the most powerful ideas of the fourth way is that the cause of negative emotions is internal, not external. This simple truth, however, has a long thread. At some point, the mind inevitably starts to blame someone or something and feel justified in doing so. This is the point where we need to abandon the urge to protect imaginary 'I' and just leap into awareness.

Negative emotions are a psychological barrier we are trying to step through. The barrier seems real but is not. As this understanding deepens, it becomes easier not to be bothered by the 'I's, not to take them personally.

If we did not identify and express negative emotions, almost everything would serve as a shock to wake us up, to make us more consciously aware. As we are, however, almost every stimulus prompts a reaction in us that puts awareness to sleep. Awareness gets immediately drawn into a subject instead of into awareness *of itself.*

Part of the art of transformation is to realize that the subject of negativity truly does not matter; that we are interested in negative emotions only for the energy behind them, and that the rest can be discarded.

One way to throw away the subject of negativity is to swallow the 'I's. This is the legendary snake consuming its own tail and thereby transcending itself.

A negative emotion is like an object the 'I's throw at us. Instead of reacting, we have to either grab the object and hold it without expressing it, or refuse to catch it in the first place and just let it fall to the ground.

Until we fully release identification with the subject (the topic, the story, the problem) behind negativity, awareness cannot achieve true independence.

Negative emotions are simply the imaginary suffering of an imaginary self or sense of ego. Conscious awareness resides beyond that as awareness of it.

A fundamental hurdle with negative emotions is the tendency to hold onto the sense of 'I' that feels wronged, and to relish the intensity of 'me' being negative which typically surges as a point of pain in our head or body. One way to slip free from this is to let the 'point' of negativity expand and circulate throughout the entire body *without visibly expressing it*, all the while observing it without criticism. This is akin to watching a ripple that is caused when a stone is thrown onto a lake. Merely watching (and feeling) the ripple spread—rather than worrying about the stone—can soften the identification, gradually neutralize it, and eventually dissolve it in the light of awareness. The end result is that the energy originally tied to a negative emotion gets transferred to and transformed as conscious awareness.

Humans have come to believe that negative emotions are an end point; a final conclusion of perception and reaction; and that there is nothing beyond it. This is untrue. There is vast internal territory beyond negative emotions. So don't stop at the negativity and the feeling of 'me' behind it. Find your way silently through the illusion of 'I'. Then step invisibly beyond it with your Self as conscious awareness. This is what Walt Whitman meant when he wrote, "All below duly travel'd, and still I mount and mount. Rise after rise bow the phantoms behind me."

Approached with right understanding, the non-expression of negative emotions is the beginning of a journey into the silent purity of conscious awareness, for which *everything* serves as fuel for transformation.

Standing outside the threshold of transformation, it is hard to realize the full significance of non-expression and transformation. Together, they bring the possibility of stepping beyond the cycle of negative emotions into a whole new realm.

Our 'person' is the owner of negative emotions and the only way to transcend them is to transcend their owner.

Transforming Negative Emotions

The fourth way talks about two conscious shocks: self-remembering and the transformation of negative emotions. The first refers to awareness stepping out of the world of thought. The second refers to awareness stepping out of the instinctive and emotional idea of 'me' which generates negative emotions.

Both conscious shocks come from the consciousness of awareness which resides outside thought and identity. In both cases, awareness realizing itself *is* the shock, just in different degrees.

Non-expression and non-identification are closely linked. The first is about not *projecting* negative emotions externally. The second is about not *becoming* them internally.

Non-expression and non-identification are aspects of the same thing. Complete non-expression requires non-identification just as non-identification requires non-expression. Ultimately they go together and serve each other as two dimensions of awareness.

Although expressing negative emotions vivifies lower centers, it rapidly dissipates awareness. The opposite is true of transformation: it dissipates identity in the lower centers and brings a rapid coalescence of awareness. It renews and restores awareness. It lifts awareness into the silent, empty realm of itself where there is no attachment to a sense of 'I'.

Negative emotions course through the bloodstream via the circuit of identification. It is as though our body becomes magnetized and electrically charged with negativity which then looks for release at the end of the circuit. In this analogy, non-expression and transformation are about closing the circuit, allowing the electrical charge to circulate freely *within*, and then channeling it to the higher socket of conscious awareness.

Non-identification neutralizes and demagnetizes negativity and brings a feeling of being relieved of a burden.

Non-expression and transformation have a physical, psychological, and metaphysical component. Non-expression is largely physical—just keeping your mouth shut—whereas examining the thinking behind negative emotions is psychological. The metaphysical aspect is when awareness consciously steps away from the physical *and* the psychological realms and is aware of being aware of watching both. This is a property, not of our physical or psychological selves, but of awareness transformed as conscious awareness.

Self-remembering means conscious awareness. Identification means unconscious awareness.

Most people have either no moments or short moments of non-identification which result in flashes or short periods of contentment and even bliss. But these moments pass with little or no clear memory of them, and with little understanding of their significance.

In rare instances, a person may unexpectedly undergo an experience in which the cable of identification is severed permanently and they discover themselves consciously free *as pure awareness*. Full comprehension of what has happened, however, depends on the person's knowledge, preparation, and experience, and the breadth of conscious awareness.

When awareness looks at negative emotions, it is looking at the psychological body.

A breakthrough happens when 'you' realize that you are not *in* a mood, but that the mood is in you. All awareness has to do is see the mood and realize itself on the outside. Then the hook is broken.

Negative emotions comprise a psychological reaction—a shield—that is intended to resist, deny, and avoid inconvenience, discomfort, pain, and loss. Awareness has to consciously move beyond this reaction and expose itself to the friction so it can leverage that as means for transformation.

The fourth way system contrasts unnecessary (imaginary) suffering with necessary (real) suffering and explains that awareness has to overcome the one to achieve the other. 'Imaginary suffering' can be seen as our psychological reaction to friction, while 'real suffering' can be seen as our conscious appropriation of friction as material for transformation.

As Mr. Ouspensky said, "negative emotions are a very low reaction." They pull awareness into our psychology and into our body. Meanwhile, the intensity behind them can fuel awareness and catapult it to conscious awareness.

Awareness cannot transcend the death of our physical body if it cannot transcend intense friction. It cannot transcend intense friction if it cannot transcend our psychological reaction to friction—negative emotions. And it cannot transcend negative emotions if it is not consciously aware of itself as awareness looking at negative emotions. This is why the first 'conscious shock' of self-remembering has to precede the second conscious shock of transforming negative emotions. There has to be something capable of not identifying with and leveraging negative emotions and then continuing to rise higher, and higher again, and again.

The human being is designed so that humanity as a whole will conform to the laws of organic life on earth. It is an enormous chain in which negative emotions play a central role. By means of the circuit of identification, imaginary 'I' produces negative emotions which create an electrical 'charge' of resistance. In this sense, imaginary 'I' is a special device in organic life designed to provide the 'shock' of negative emotions. Whenever we identify with, indulge in, and express negative emotions, we join with this circuit and contribute to this shock. In doing so, we primarily serve the laws of the moon which *depends* on humanity identifying with friction and suffering.

At the same time, the human being is also designed as an incubator for awareness; as a cocoon in which awareness can coalesce and consciously realize itself. Here, too, identification and negative emotions play a central role. For it is by neutralizing the conduit of identification, unplugging the current of negative emotions, and absorbing suffering that awareness consciously fortifies itself as awareness. Through this process, awareness breaks free from the pull of the moon, assumes a positive 'charge' unto itself, and becomes eligible for ascension in the Ray of Creation.

Negative emotions can be extremely fast, yet they do not exist in the present. They buffer, deflect, resist, deny—negate—what happens in the present as a *reaction*. The origin of this reaction can stretch back seconds, minutes, hours, days, or years as negative emotions hang onto and prolong themselves by dwelling on a reaction, revisiting it, exaggerating it, feeding it. But what they are really holding onto and feeding as an imaginary sense of 'I' and 'me'.

Negative emotions exist in time (as perceived by the lower centers) whereas conscious awareness exists outside the phenomenon of time as the container of time—as the void in which the present moment eternally emerges. Transformation is a plunge into this void which has no identity and no destination yet is full of awareness that is conscious of being aware as infinite awareness.

In the end, comprehending transformation is not fully possible for lower centers and negative emotions can never be completely resolved on their own level. Transformation means "changing form" and "metamorphosing" from a psychological sense of 'I' to a metaphysical state of awareness. It marks the transition from a lower dimension to a higher dimension that is the exclusive domain of conscious awareness.

Transforming Negative Emotions

www.ingramcontent.com/pod-product-compliance
Lightning Source LLC
Chambersburg PA
CBHW020656300426
44112CB00007B/402